June—
With Love
and Thanks
all you do—
Wayne

VINEYARD SUMMER

. . . .

VINEYARD SUMMER

. . . .

PHOTOGRAPHS BY
ALISON SHAW

~

WITH A FOREWORD BY
RICHARD RESTON

LITTLE, BROWN AND COMPANY ~ BOSTON NEW YORK TORONTO LONDON

FIRST EDITION

Library of Congress Cataloging-in-Publication Data

Shaw, Alison.
    Vineyard summer / photographs by Alison Shaw with a foreword
by Richard Reston. — 1st ed.
        p.   cm.
    ISBN 0-316-78345-5
    1. Martha's Vineyard (Mass.) — Pictorial works. 2. Summer —
Massachusetts — Martha's Vineyard — Pictorial works. I. Title.
F72.M5S485   1994
779'.9974494 — dc20   93-43504

10 9 8 7 6 5 4 3 2 1

NIL

Book design by Sue Dawson
with Barbara Werden

Published simultaneously in Canada by Little, Brown & Company
(Canada) Limited

PRINTED IN ITALY

FOREWORD

. . . .

BY RICHARD RESTON

WHEN I first met Alison Shaw, I had just arrived on Martha's Vineyard to take over as editor of the *Vineyard Gazette,* then a nearly 130-year-old newspaper recognized as one of the oldest and finest regional community papers in the United States. That was nineteen years ago. Alison, a recent graduate of Smith College, had moved to the Island a few months earlier and was working two days a week as an inserter in the production department of the *Gazette.* And then one day she walked into my office and asked that I give her a chance to publish her photography in the paper.

That conversation began what would turn into a remarkable career for this young photographer. Her early work for the *Gazette* was rough, by her own admission. But she worked long and extra hours, often in her spare time, taking pictures and processing film, in those days laboring out of an old kitchen converted for use as the *Gazette* darkroom.

Today Alison Shaw continues to record with her camera the life and times of this extraordinary Island community for the *Gazette.* Her responsibilities, however, extend far beyond the role of photographer, for which she is best known. She is in charge now of the graphics and layout of the newspaper, a position critical to the look and character of the old *Gazette.* She designs *Martha's Vineyard Magazine,* a quarterly color publication owned by the *Gazette.* Indeed, in almost everything the *Gazette* publishes these days, from special editions to summer tourist guides, Alison's influence is deeply felt, partly because of her background in art history and largely because of her special skills as a photographer and graphic designer.

She remains more innovative and more experimental than most of her colleagues, the result not only of long years of hard work but of rare personal commitment to the art of photography. The *Vineyard Gazette,* I believe, has played an enormous role in the development of Alison Shaw. It seeks to protect the fragile resources of this Island by calling public attention to the beauty around us, by underscoring the

. . . .

qualities of life that forever will be worthy of conservation and preservation. It is this mission, this spirit, that Alison's camera catches with mood and a precision that sets her apart from other photographers.

The testimony lies ahead in the pages of this glorious book, *Vineyard Summer.* And there can be no doubt for those who read on about the special place Alison Shaw commands today in the world of photography, a world that begins on Martha's Vineyard but reaches far beyond these Island boundaries. Her recognition within art circles these days comes from across the nation, from Island and mainland exhibits, from her many invitations to teach, from volumes of work published in newspapers and magazines. Shaw's photography now hangs permanently in countless public and private places, from art galleries to corporate businesses to the homes of collectors. President Clinton returned to the White House with an Alison Shaw landscape after a trip to the Vineyard.

Vineyard Summer makes clear what so many on Martha's Vineyard and elsewhere in the country have known for a long while, that Alison Shaw simply stands apart as one of the brighter talents in today's younger generation of leading photographers.

Her second book of photography, *Vineyard Summer* represents a bold and wholly new step for Shaw. Now, in this book, the photographer enters for the first time the dramatic world of color, a critical juncture for an artist better known in years past for her black-and-white work. "This book has been brewing in me for the last three or four years, really since color photography began to take hold and play a more central and dominant role in my work," Shaw says. "*Vineyard Summer* is a more current representation of my photography; it's what I'm in the middle of, not just an anthology of the best of my past work. I shot pictures for *Vineyard Summer* right up to deadline.

"The book is a doubling up, partly a book about the Vineyard, partly an art book. Its aim is to reflect the Island, to reinforce the sense of place, while reaching out beyond the Vineyard, beyond location, through the use of photography as art. I look for that special quality of Island light that brings out color, intense colors. I am looking for scenes and subjects with saturated color," the photographer says.

"There aren't many other places in the world like this Island where I can take my camera and work with reflections off the water at both dawn and dusk. The Vineyard is one little piece of earth, specifically defined, and my present excitement with color photography allows me new horizons, different ways of exploring the Island, particularly after fifteen years of working mainly in black-and-white.

"The sheer energy of color has opened my eyes again."

One thing Alison Shaw will never be accused of is practicing her art with jaded eyes. She remains as fresh and enthusiastic in her color work for *Vineyard Summer* as she was in *Remembrance and Light,* her first book, done in black-and-white ten years ago. The reader will see in this book something more than a collection of beautiful pictures.

Shaw's camera is used in this case not to produce a guide or travel book about Martha's Vineyard but to define and capture the spirit of an Island she loves, of a place she has called home for nearly twenty years.

Every artist – photographer, painter, writer – draws on some center for inspiration, for creative energy. And for Shaw that center clearly lies in the community of Martha's Vineyard, in the chemistry and quality of Island life, in the character of its human landscape, and in the lovely but fragile look of the Vineyard environment. The Island remains the central platform for Shaw's main body of work, and this photographer is always at her best when she is closest to the natural world of Martha's Vineyard. She defines the art of her photography in Vineyard terms, and she talks and thinks of the Island even when working elsewhere in the country – the shooting of a sunset in San Francisco, the landscape of a dawn along the Florida coast.

Readers of *Vineyard Summer* will understand why Alison Shaw has captured just about every top prize in New England journalism. They also will recognize that this is an important book, both for what it says about Shaw's work in color and for what it tells us about the spirit and character of this Vineyard that so colors her photography.

The photographer's camera will carry you to extraordinary Island settings, to the twinkling of ferryboat lights caught in the shimmer of a still harbor at dawn, to the beauty and bounty of a farmers' market, to a gull skimming low across the foam of whitecaps, to the high ocean skies and shifting dunes of the Vineyard's great south coast. Shaw gives you special glimpses of Island detail, a red buoy in a blue chair, the stripes of a bright beach umbrella, an ornate stained glass window, a field of blowing wildflowers, the candlelight of lanterns on Illumination Night in the old Oak Bluffs Camp Grounds.

These photographs in *Vineyard Summer* measure time and change within a single Island season. They are photographs but also paintings, lichen on an old stone wall after a rainfall, sweeps of sunset and sunrise, reflections of color at water's edge, the majesty of Vineyard lighthouses, the humor of Island children. There is little that escapes Shaw's camera. She has an uncanny ability to compose and print pictures that most other photographers might never see.

Vineyard Summer is an important book because it not only records the life of an unusual Island community but also provides a study of the remarkable skills of a superb photographer. Alison Shaw says she is now only in the middle of this period of her color photography. And so one can only imagine where she will turn next for an encore to such a glorious middle.

VINEYARD SUMMER

· · · · · · · · · · · ·

NORTH SHORE, 1990

MENEMSHA, 1991

ISLANDER, VINEYARD HAVEN HARBOR, 1991

YELLOW TULIPS, VINEYARD HAVEN, 1993

MILL POND, WEST TISBURY, 1990

WEST TISBURY, 1993

9

STONE WALL, BEETLEBUNG CORNER, 1993

POPPIES, MARINA'S FIELD, 1993

FARMERS' MARKET, 1992

12

AGRICULTURAL FAIR, WEST TISBURY, 1993

GREEN BOAT, 1991

14

GREEN BOAT, MENEMSHA, 1990

GANNON & BENJAMIN BOATYARD, 1992

PAUL'S POINT, 1993

ISLANDER, VINEYARD HAVEN HARBOR, 1992

18

BIG BRIDGE, 1992
....

BEACH ROAD, 1992

LAGOON, 1990

23

RED BUOY, EDGARTOWN HARBOR, 1992

RED BOAT, EDGARTOWN HARBOR, 1992

25

YELLOW BOAT, 1992

PURPLE DOOR, CIRCUIT AVENUE, 1992

SUNFLOWERS, TIASQUAM BROOK FARM, 1992

YELLOW BOAT, COW BAY, 1991

LEMONS, FARMERS' MARKET, 1993

30

Red tulip, Oak Bluffs, 1992

TOMATOES, FARM POND HOUSE, 1993

PEPPERS, FARMERS' MARKET, 1993

34

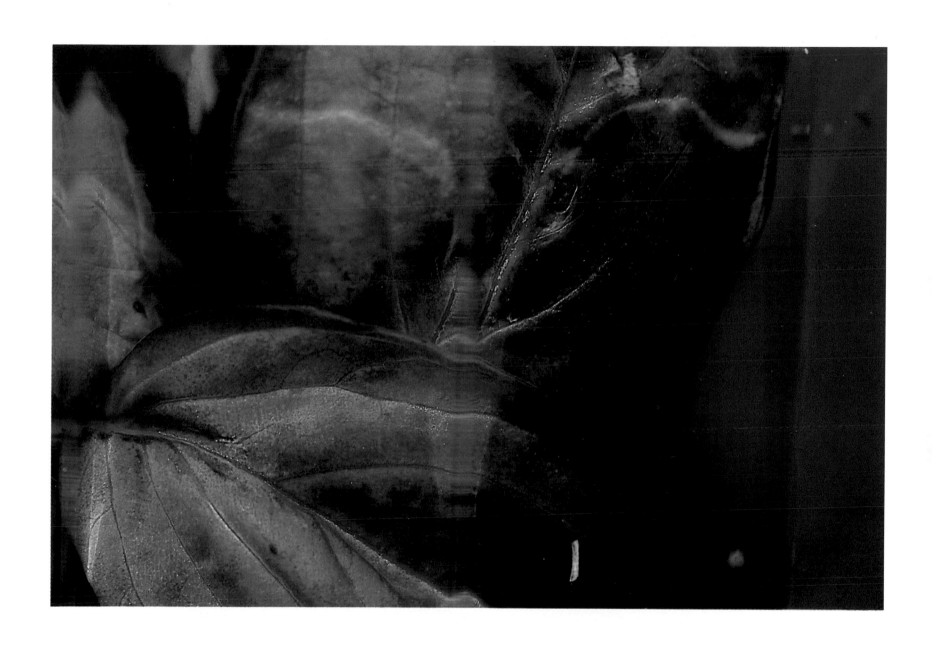

BASIL AND RED PEPPERS, FARMERS' MARKET, 1993

Red Tricycle, 1993

T-SHIRT, EDGARTOWN, 1993

EDGARTOWN YACHT CLUB, 1993

UMBRELLA, MENEMSHA BEACH, 1993

39

SWIMMING TRUNKS, BEND IN THE ROAD BEACH, 1993

ELIAS PEPPER, STATE BEACH, 1992

CHILMARK, 1993
....

42

EAST CHOP LIGHTHOUSE, 1991

STONEWALL BEACH, 1993

OYSTER POND, 1990

FARM POND CHANNEL, 1990
················

OAK HOUSE, 1993

Sweetened Water Farm, 1989

SOUTH SHORE, 1989

FARM POND, 1991

LUCY VINCENT BEACH, 1991

NANTUCKET SOUND, 1992

Black Dog Tavern, 1992

HARTHAVEN HARBOR, 1991

OCEAN PARK FIREWORKS, 1992

Ocean Park Fireworks, 1992

FLYING HORSES, 1991

FLYING HORSES RESTORATION, RALEIGH, NORTH CAROLINA, 1991

Oyster Bar, 1993

ILLUMINATION NIGHT, CAMP GROUNDS, 1992

RED TULIPS, EDGARTOWN, 1993

GREEN LEAVES, KATAMA AVENUE, 1993

BLUEBERRIES, FARMERS' MARKET, 1993

RADISHES, FARMERS' MARKET, 1993

FARMERS' MARKET, 1992

PINK HOUSE, CAMP GROUNDS, 1993

MENEMSHA, 1993

MENEMSHA, 1992

GAY HEAD BEACH, 1993

PAUL'S POINT, 1990

LUCY VINCENT BEACH, 1991

STATE BEACH, 1992

SENGEKONTACKET, 1991

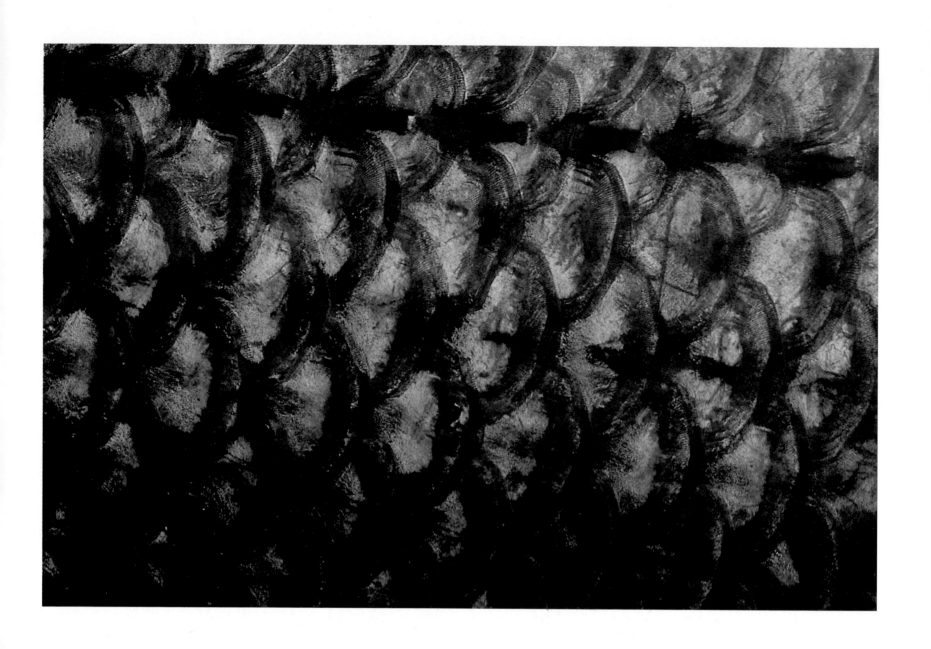

STRIPED BASS, POOLE'S FISH MARKET, 1990

HERRING RUN, GAY HEAD, 1992

MENEMSHA, 1990
· · · · · · · · · · · · ·

MENEMSHA, 1991

MENEMSHA, 1990

MENEMSHA, 1992

NORTH SHORE, 1990

SPLIT ROCK, MAKONIKEY, 1990

GAY HEAD, 1990

WHITING FARM, 1991

86

VINEYARD SOUND, 1990

VIOLET, VINEYARD HAVEN HARBOR, 1993

BEACH UMBRELLAS, 1992

90

EAST CHOP LIGHTHOUSE, 1991

RED OARS, 1991

Red boat, Menemsha, 1990

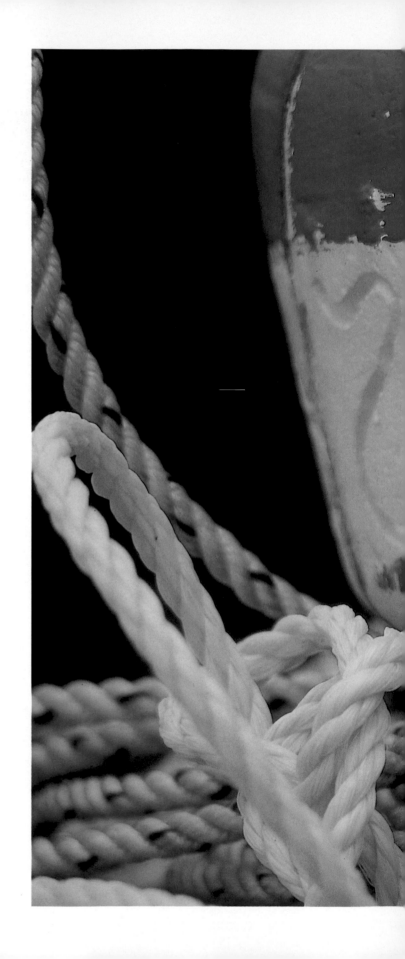

Yellow buoys, Menemsha, 1993

OCEAN PARK, 1993

OCEAN PARK, 1993

Squash blossoms, Farmers' Market, 1993

FARMERS' MARKET, 1992

MARINA'S FIELD, 1990

EMILY POST HOUSE, EDGARTOWN, 1993

OYSTER POND, 1990

EASTVILLE, 1993

NORTH ROAD, 1992

EDGARTOWN LIGHTHOUSE, 1992

FRESNEL LENS, VINEYARD MUSEUM, 1992

HARTHAVEN HARBOR, 1993

BEND IN THE ROAD BEACH, 1993

Inkwell Beach, 1993

MAKONIKEY, 1993

MENEMSHA TEXACO, 1993

112

MENEMSHA, 1993

GAY HEAD LIGHTHOUSE, 1992

Notes

· · · · · · · · · · · ·

I'VE BEEN TAKING PHOTOGRAPHS on Martha's Vineyard for nearly twenty years. As a child I spent summers here, staying in my grandparents' house in Edgartown. I moved to the Island after graduating from college and have lived here year-round ever since.

Living on an island has been my greatest inspiration. I love the fact that such specific boundaries define an island. These boundaries force me constantly to explore the Vineyard anew with my camera, to look at the same things in new ways. Over the years, this has taken my work from documentary to abstract, and from black-and-white to mostly color.

Most of the photographs in this book were taken with a Nikon 35mm camera, usually my F-3. I also used a Pentax 6 x 7 medium-format camera for many of the panoramic landscapes.

When I'm working in 35mm, I normally carry a couple of camera bodies – one for color, one for black-and-white – and a whole range of lenses, from a 20mm up to a 300mm. My preferred lens for landscapes is a 24mm or 28mm, or the equivalent in medium format. Either lens is useful in capturing the sweeping effect of a landscape. Other lenses I use frequently are 55mm, 105mm, and 200mm. The two extremes of 20mm and 300mm are there when I need them, but I don't think any of the pictures in this book were taken with those lenses.

My film of choice is Fujichrome transparency film, which does a great job with vivid colors. I rarely use filters. What I'm drawn to when I'm shooting is colors and light already present in the picture. So it's not a matter of creating an effect, but of recording it.

I nearly always use a tripod – mine is a Gitzo with a Bogen quick-release head – when I'm photographing in color. A sturdy tripod is an invaluable tool for shooting with slow film speeds. It also allows me to experiment with long exposures and gives me the ability to frame compositions accurately through the viewfinder. The images in this book are virtually all uncropped.

The following are some of the stories behind selected photographs from *Vineyard Summer.*

Page 11, POPPIES, MARINA'S FIELD, 1993

Marina's Field is a breathtaking field of wildflowers in Chilmark. It is one of my favorite places to take pictures at the height of summer. Early morning is the best time to find the blossoms perfectly still, but I don't like to be too early, because the warm yellow color of early-morning light muddies the trueness of the color green. On the morning I took this picture, it was an intensely moving and almost mystical experience to find myself surrounded by a sea of bright red poppies. I set up my tripod and my Pentax right in the middle of the field and took pictures until I ran out of film. I finally left at 8:00 A.M., feeling both emotionally exhilarated and exhausted.

Page 13, AGRICULTURAL FAIR, WEST TISBURY, 1993

President Clinton and his family arrived on a Thursday afternoon in August for a ten-day vacation on the Island. We worked straight through the night Thursday to put out a special edition of the *Vineyard Gazette* to welcome the First Family. Friday morning, with the paper on the newsstands, I decided it was more important to try to photograph the president than to catch up on my sleep. Much of my time in the days that followed was spent waiting for him, following him, and guessing where on the Island he'd go next. Since we thought it was a sure bet that the president would make an appearance at the Agricultural Fair in West Tisbury, that's where I headed that Friday morning. It took many hours of "hanging out" time, over two days, before I, along with thousands of fairgoers and hundreds of other journalists, was finally rewarded with a presidential visit late Saturday afternoon. It was such a wild and chaotic scene when he did arrive, however, that the pictures I took were barely worth printing. But having all that time to kill left me with plenty of opportunity to look for other pictures, including this photograph of a prizewinning sheep. I waited for just the right combination of right-side-up ribbons in crisp focus (they were constantly fluttering and turning in the wind). And the sheep needed to be visible through the fence but far enough in the background that he would be softly out of focus. By the way, this sheep won first prize in the "Fat Sheep" category.

Page 15, GREEN BOAT, MENEMSHA, 1990

I love playing with the colorful reflections of boats in the water. It's a tricky shot to get. First, there's a lot left up to chance; since the reflections are constantly moving, no two images are the same. Then there's the choice of what to focus on: the boat, its reflection, or the surface of the water. If I want all three, which I usually do (particularly because there's rarely an obvious center of interest), I've got to be sure I'm in plenty of bright sunlight so that I can use a small enough f-stop to have maximum depth of field. It doesn't help matters any that I'm normally using a long 200mm lens to try to isolate a detail of a boat and its reflection. Then there's the problem of motion — since the water is always moving, I need a fast enough shutter speed (a minimum of 1/125 second) to freeze that motion. So I try for the best of everything, with bright sun to give me as small an f-stop and as fast a shutter speed as I can manage. The last thing I'd want to do here is go with a much faster film speed. What I would gain in depth of field and shutter speed would not be worth the sacrifice in color saturation.

Page 21, BEACH ROAD, 1992

After Hurricane Bob, dump trucks removed much of the sand that had washed onto the parking lots at South Beach and deposited a load at a time to help restore the ravaged shoreline along Beach Road. These neat piles of sand made for an interesting silhouette at dawn. Day after day I set my alarm clock for 5:00 A.M., hoping for crystal-clear skies. In the meantime, the piles of sand gradually began to settle and lose their graceful contour. Finally, the perfect clear morning came when the line of little manmade dunes, although somewhat diminished, still formed a pretty shape and I was able to get my photograph.

Pages 22–23, LAGOON, 1990

The head of the Lagoon is my favorite place to photograph early in the morning on those spring or fall days when the nights get very cool but the days stay quite warm. When the night is still and the temperature drops far enough, a mist forms over the water, sometimes even billowing up as far as the treetops. It sits there, nestled in the hollow between shores, until the sun climbs high enough to burn it off.

Page 25, RED BOAT, EDGARTOWN HARBOR, 1992

Last summer, while I was showing my work at a gallery, a woman asked me how I got my colors. Did I use filters? Did I use darkroom tricks? I explained that it was by and large a matter of *finding* the colors and simply recording them on film. She seemed skeptical, so I told her the next time she found herself by the Edgartown wharf on a bright sunny afternoon around two o'clock or so, she should look at the fishing boats tied up along the dock and carefully examine their reflections in the water. Well, at my next show, the same woman came up to me, very excited, saying, "I saw it. I saw what you were talking about." The only trick was seeing it in the first place.

Page 33, TOMATOES, FARM POND HOUSE, 1993

Often the best photographs can be found in the most ordinary or unexpected places. Things in my own house or yard catch my eye. These are homegrown tomatoes, which we had put in a colander on the kitchen counter with a Post-it note stating "Photo prop – DO NOT EAT." I finally found the time a week later to take this picture of the tomatoes on my front doorstep. The photograph on the facing page is of a lone tulip that turned up in my garden several years ago. I photographed it early in the morning after a soft rainfall, surrounding it with sheets of white foamcore, which doubled as both windbreaks and reflectors.

Page 34, PEPPERS, FARMERS' MARKET, 1993

I fell in love with this basket of peppers at the Farmers' Market. It was overcast and had been misting lightly that Saturday morning. The dull light, the moisture, and Fujichrome's way with the color green all helped make the peppers come alive.

Page 39, UMBRELLA, MENEMSHA BEACH, 1993

There was a crisp blue sky this day, with a few fluffy white clouds floating around, and I was in search of a good umbrella — I truly do spend considerable time driving around looking for good beach umbrellas. This day I found one on the beach at Menemsha. I asked the two women who were quietly enjoying their picnic lunch in the shade of the umbrella whether they'd mind if I took a picture. I proceeded to spend the next half hour scooting around in the sand on my stomach trying to find a good angle, shooting several rolls of film, while the women occasionally eyed me curiously.

Page 46, FARM POND CHANNEL, 1990

The morning I took this picture, I woke up early and looked out my bedroom window at this amazing bank of clouds. I immediately jumped out of bed, donned sweatpants, shirt, and boots right over my pajamas, and was on location, knee-deep in salt water, in less than five minutes. I knew the band of clouds was moving fast, the sun was rising all too quickly, and in another five minutes I would have missed the shot.

Page 49, SOUTH SHORE, 1989

I had wanted to take a photograph of this particular stretch of shoreline for quite some time but needed the right light in order to make my picture. On this afternoon a front had gone through, and I could see that three days of dreary, rainy weather were about to give way to clear air and bright sunshine. As the clouds began to break up, I made a mad dash for my location – clear across the Island and then down a three-mile dirt road, all the while racing against the clock and against the clouds. If I remember correctly, I was actually loading film into the camera as I drove, not something I'd necessarily recommend. When I arrived at the beach, I had just enough time to set up my tripod and make three exposures in fairly rapid succession. To give you an idea of how fast the cloudbank was moving, in the first exposure the clouds filled the top of the frame, and in the third exposure they were merely a distant band near the horizon. This photograph is the middle exposure. The warm reddish glow comes from both the late-afternoon light and the Kodachrome film.

Four years after I took *South Shore,* President Clinton visited the Island. The beach in front of the house where he stayed was this exact same stretch of shoreline, so I thought a personally inscribed, framed print of *South Shore* might make a nice gift and reminder of his Martha's Vineyard vacation. I was lucky enough to present the photograph myself to President and Mrs. Clinton and Chelsea at the Granary Gallery in West Tisbury.

Page 56, OCEAN PARK FIREWORKS, 1992

The annual Oak Bluffs fireworks are just about the best display I've seen, anytime, anyplace. Fireworks are actually very easy to photograph. Just pick the right f-stop – in my case that's approximately f-8 for 50 speed film – mount your camera on a sturdy tripod, set your shutter speed on bulb, and

then, when you make your exposure, leave the shutter open for as long as the fireworks seem interesting.

Page 57, OCEAN PARK FIREWORKS, 1992

A whole different way to photograph a fireworks display is to turn around and look at the crowd. The light cast by the different-colored fireworks created an eerie and magical glow, well worth a picture.

Page 59, FLYING HORSES RESTORATION, 1991

Oak Bluffs is home to the country's oldest operating carousel, the Flying Horses. Several years ago, all of the horses spent the winter months undergoing restoration in Raleigh, North Carolina. I visited them for a couple of days in Raleigh and photographed them in various stages of repair. It was fascinating to watch as Rosa Ragan, the woman who did the work on the horses, chipped away layer after layer of old paint, using nothing but a heat gun and a small knife. This horse, which lies on Rosa's worktable in her brick studio, is nearly stripped of its old paint. The warm glow comes from the tungsten light source. The photograph on the facing page is of a restored horse, back at home on the carousel in Oak Bluffs.

Page 63, GREEN LEAVES, KATAMA AVENUE, 1993

A couple of months ago I was teaching a photography student about depth of field, shutter speeds, exposure, reciprocity failure, spot metering, and how they all relate. I took her into my backyard and picked this branch of a maple tree as our subject matter. I set her camera on a tripod and had her run through all sorts of variations of f-stops and shutter speeds. We experimented with time exposures, letting the wind blow the branch, or moving it ourselves, or moving it for only a portion of the exposure. We used a polarizing filter as a neutral density filter to increase the length of the exposure and then adjusted the exposure to account for the film's reciprocity failure. I pointed out that even though the background of this photograph consisted of the basement level of my neighbor's house, all you would see would be a nice solid black, since it was in shadow and our main exposure was taken off the brightly backlit leaves. A week later we got my student's slides back from the lab, and I flipped over how gorgeous and painterly they were. I immediately went back out in the yard with my own camera and had a wonderful time repeating all the experiments myself.

Page 65, RADISHES, FARMERS' MARKET, 1993

The Farmers' Market in West Tisbury is my favorite summer event to photograph. For one thing, I love the fact that it takes place every week, giving me a chance to go back again and again. I also love to see how quickly the produce comes into season and then, just as quickly, goes out of season. For example, there's just a single Saturday morning of the summer when the radishes are at their peak, as in this photograph. And the same is true of the strawberries, the tomatoes, and the sunflowers. I usually try to reach the market early, before it opens. The vendors are very friendly about my poking around with my camera before the buying public arrives. On the morning of this bright harvest of radishes, I didn't arrive until after the market was already under way and thus had to contend with constantly losing my subject matter to eager customers. It was a challenge squeezing in 8-second exposures – the morning was dark and spitting rain – amid a pressing crowd of shoppers.

Page 83, SPLIT ROCK, MAKONIKEY, 1990

What launched me into a serious pursuit of color photography was the *Vineyard Gazette*'s decision to purchase the four-color, glossy *Martha's Vineyard Magazine* in the late spring of 1990. Suddenly, color photography went from being a vacation activity to being a job. (But not a job in the traditional sense – it's really much more like a hobby that I get paid for!) Rather than having the leisure of taking pictures on vacation, I was suddenly under deadline pressure to produce color photographs for publication. This picture of Split Rock at Makonikey is from my first assignment for *Martha's Vineyard Magazine* – to photograph the Island's North Shore. It was taken just before dark, using a long exposure with my Pentax mounted on a tripod. I believe that the very slight bluish-green cast was caused by a processing error, which happily improved the picture.

Page 86, WHITING FARM, 1991

In early spring, I was photographing lambs for a photo essay to appear in *Martha's Vineyard Magazine*. Over a couple of weeks' time, most mornings I would go early to Whiting Farm in West Tisbury to see the new lambs. I found myself mesmerized, watching them for hours at a time. For the lambs, playing mostly involved racing around the pen in groups, first one way, then the other, leaping in the air, and generally driving their mothers crazy. With a 105mm lens, and my camera set on a slow shutter speed, I tried my best to follow this activity by panning the lambs, a difficult task to accomplish, since their movement was so random. I think this photograph captures some of their exuberance.

Page 87, VINEYARD SOUND, 1990

Herring gulls follow the ferries back and forth across Vineyard Sound, partly for sport and partly in search of Fritos, pretzels, and other assorted delicacies tossed from the deck by well-meaning tourists. This photograph was taken with a slowish shutter speed – probably 1/60 second – while I leaned over the rail and followed the gull's flight with my camera. It's tricky to match the gull's speed and direction, taking into account the motion of the ferry as well. There's a lot of luck involved, and for every one of these shots that really works I probably throw out the thirty-five others on the roll.

Pages 88–89, VIOLET, VINEYARD HAVEN HARBOR, 1993

While sailing on the gaff-rig ketch *Violet* across Vineyard Sound, I was escorted by the captain to a precarious perch at the end of the bowsprit. Friends who invited me along for the sail were getting great enjoyment from watching me nervously hang on to the bowsprit with one hand while clutching my camera in the other. The F-3 luckily has a motor drive, making one-handed operation a little easier. As my friends snapped their own pictures of me, I reciprocated, until suddenly I realized that snapshots of my pals taking pictures of me probably wouldn't make for such great book material. They were happy to cooperate, discreetly tucking themselves aft, so I could grab this photograph, taken with a 24mm lens. The wide-angle lens enhances the sense of perspective and makes the image appear a bit distorted.

Pages 110–111, MAKONIKEY, 1993

This picture was taken with my Pentax 6 x 7. I like using the larger-format camera when I'm trying to capture such smooth and subtle gradations of tone and color. It was at dusk on a crystal-clear, nearly still night. I stopped the lens down almost all the way to increase the length of the exposure. I remember that this particular exposure was about six minutes, giving the water a chance to wash over itself again and again, creating the soft sensation of a fine mist suspended over the water. Since the sky was far brighter than the water, I used a piece of black cardboard, which I held directly in front of the lens and moved rapidly up and down at roughly the level of the horizon, to hold back exposure from the sky and therefore more evenly balance it with the exposure of the water.

THANK YOU TO MY EDITORS AND COLLEAGUES at the *Vineyard Gazette* for putting up with my many temporary disappearances from the world of print journalism and black-and-white photography in order to devote time to this book. Two colleagues in particular stand out. Dick Reston has supported and guided my photography over the nineteen years we've worked together. It was only fitting that he write the Foreword for *Vineyard Summer*. And Amy Callahan was always there to offer help with writing, editing, typing, and moral support. Special thanks to all of the Islanders, year-round and summer, who have encouraged my photography over the years. Thanks also to my editor, Jennifer Josephy, for making *Vineyard Summer* possible. And thank you, most especially, to Sue Dawson, for all of her design work, the long hours spent leaning over light tables peering at thousands of images, the late-night and early-morning hours spent staring into computer screens with only coffee to keep us going, as well as the time spent waiting patiently in my car while I took "just one more picture."